Paul D. Pointer

YO-CXL-024

(Written in:1995, Age: 11)

© P2Productions LLC
Made in the United States of America

Editor: Paul Pointer / Illustrator: Paul Pointer / Author: Paul Pointer

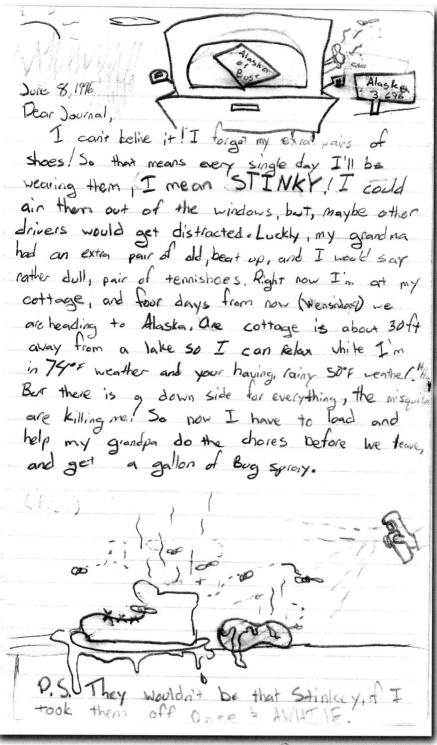

June 8, 1996

Dear Journal,

I can't belive it! I forgot my extra pairs of shoes! So that means every single day I'll be wearing them, I mean STINKY! I could air them out of the windows, but, maybe other drivers would get distracted. Luckly, my grandma had an extra pair of old, beat up, and I would say rather dull, pair of tennishoes. Right now I'm at my cottage, and four days from now (Wensnday) we are heading to Alaska. Our cottage is about 30ft away from a lake so I can relax while I'm in 74°F weather and your haying, rainy 50°F weather. Ha ha! But there is a down side for everything, the misquito are killing me! So now I have to load and help my grandpa do the chores before we leave, and get a gallon of Bug spray.

P.S. They wouldn't be that Stinkey, if I took them off Once A AWHILE.

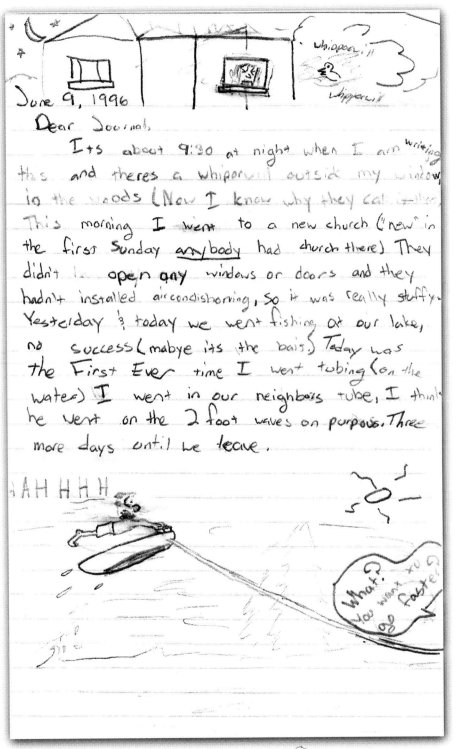

June 9, 1996

Dear Journal,

It's about 9:30 at night when I am writing this and theres a whiperwil outside my window in the woods (Now I know why they call it that) This morning I went to a new church ("new" in the first Sunday anybody had church there) They didn't open any windows or doors and they hadn't installed aircondishoning, so it was really stuffy. Yesterday & today we went fishing at our lake, no success (mabye its the bait) Today was the First Ever time I went tubing (on the water) I went in our neighbors tube, I think he went on the 2 foot waves on purpous. Three more days until we leave.

June 10, 1996

Dear Journal,

Today was a long day, a very humid 82°F weather day. The highlights of my day were: having a wood tick on my neck, watching the <u>Cat From Outer Space</u>, having 5 misquto bites on my forehead in a 2 cm radius, & writing this journal. Two more days.

(Dramazation)

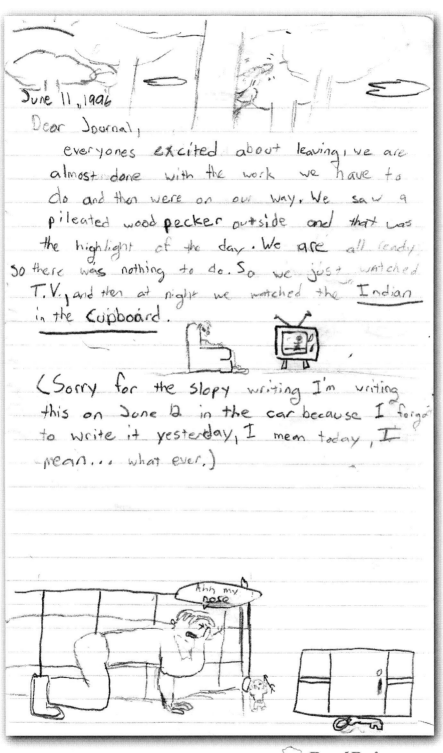

June 11, 1996

Dear Journal,

everyones excited about leaving, we are almost done with the work we have to do and then were on our way. We saw a pileated wood pecker outside and that was the highlight of the day. We are all ready, so there was nothing to do. So we just watched T.V., and then at night we watched the Indian in the Cupboard.

(Sorry for the slopy writing I'm writing this on June 12 in the car because I forgot to write it yesterday, I mean today, I mean... what ever.)

Ahh my nose

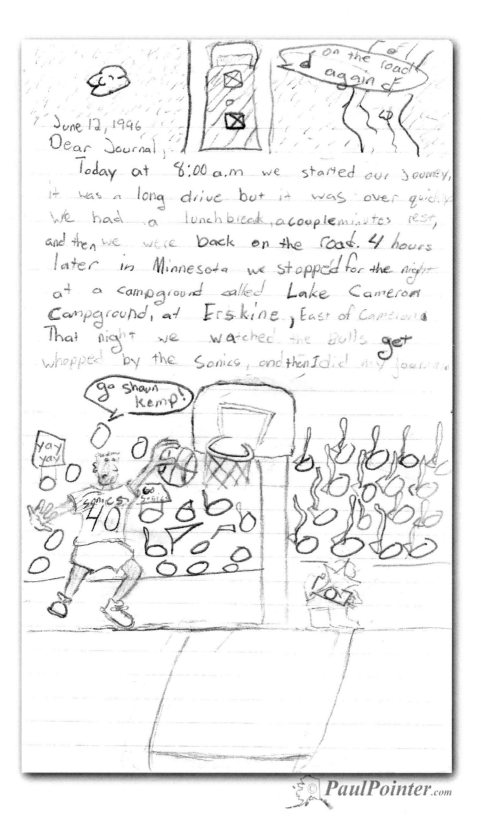

June 12, 1996

Dear Journal,

Today at 8:00 a.m we started our journey, it was a long drive but it was over quickly. We had a lunch break, a couple minutes rest, and then we were back on the road. 4 hours later in Minnesota we stopped for the night at a campground called Lake Cameron Campground, at Erskine, East of Cameron. That night we watched the Bulls get whopped by the Sonics, and then I did my journal.

June 13, 1996

Dear Journal,

We started off from the camp ground at 8:30 and headed to North Dakoda. We did some more driving, and then had lunch. (driving is not as boring as it seems, we usally just play games, read a book, or just admire the scenery) We saw two seagulls (hard to belive) you would think that they would be a huge body of water. (Like 'lake' Michagan.) We also fed a Columbian ground squirl some chips. Then we did some more driving and came to a town in North Dakota Called, Tioga. We stayed there for the night, and watched a baseball game in their feild.

North Dakota

Huh?

Let's Play Ball!

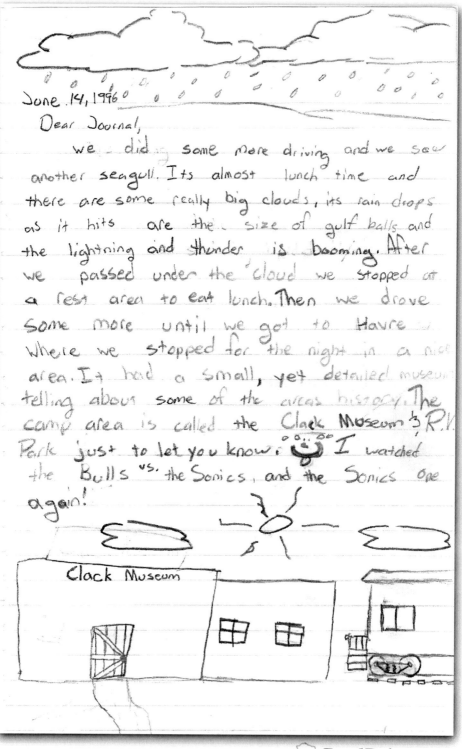

June 14, 1996

Dear Journal,

We did some more driving and we saw another seagull. Its almost lunch time and there are some really big clouds, its rain drops as it hits are the size of gulf balls and the lightning and thunder is booming. After we passed under the cloud we stopped at a rest area to eat lunch. Then we drove some more until we got to Havre where we stopped for the night in a nice area. It had a small, yet detailed museum telling about some of the areas history. The camp area is called the Clack Museum & R.V. Park just to let you know. ☺ I watched the Bulls vs. the Sonics, and the Sonics one again!

Clack Museum

Wheel of Fortune!

June 15, 1996

Dear Journal,

we have the Wheel of Fortune hand held video game! Dun, Dun, Dun. cool huh. We are in Montana and the are some really gigantic mountains out here. We are stopping at Glacier National park, where there is glaciers that have been here for thousands of years. And right next door is the Continental Divide (the Rocky Mountains). We are staying here for two days. These Mountains are humungos! We have it on my grandpas video tape and boy are they gorgoos. We are at an elevation at about 5,000 feet and the mountains in the videotape are about 10,000 feet. We saw 3 columbian ground squirls today, they wanted our popcorn. I wish you could see this spectacular scenery, just magnificent.

Continental Divide

we are here

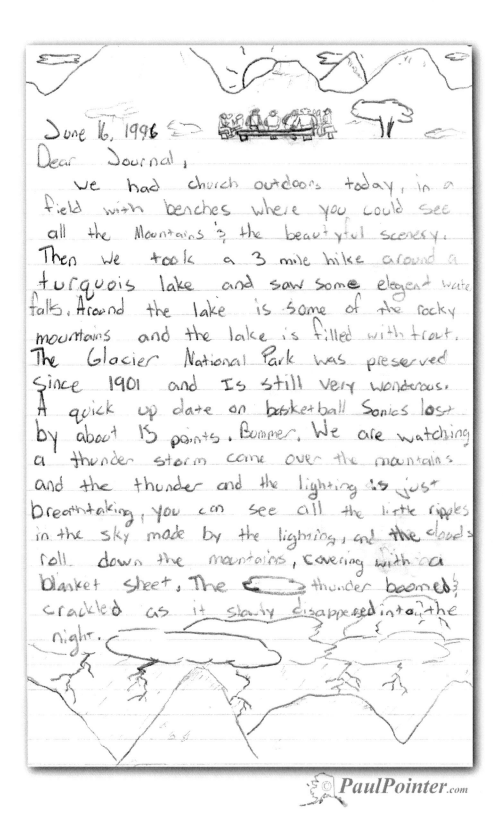

June 16, 1996

Dear Journal,

We had church outdoors today, in a field with benches where you could see all the Mountains & the beautyful scenery. Then we took a 3 mile hike around a turquois lake and saw some elegent water falls. Around the lake is some of the rocky mountains and the lake is filled with trout. The Glacier National Park was preserved since 1901 and Is still very wonderous. A quick up date on basketball Sonics lost by about 15 points. Bummer. We are watching a thunder storm come over the mountains and the thunder and the lighting is just breathtaking, you can see all the little ripples in the sky made by the lighting, and the clouds roll down the mountains, covering with a blanket sheet. The thunder boomed & crackled as it slowly disappered into the night.

U.S. | Canada

June 17, 1996

Dear Journal,

   Today were in another country Canada, and its almost like your in France but there is mountains all around. Were in the Alberta Province, and its alot colder. We saw a badger today at the gulf course (I guess there still is a little of Wisconsin following me around.) We going to gulf tommoro (actually I should say my Grandpa does I catty, but I know enough to play.) We went to the Prince of Whales hotel and it is very fansy and huge. My Grandpa and I found gold & we scaled a rocky cliff. The cliff was only 12 feet but it was made of entirely of rocks, and you have to be very, very strong to climb it. (kidding) The gold we found was a kodak **Gold** camera, that some one had left at the rivers edge. (you might think that its warm here, but guess again)

Which is Gold
Column A and, or B.

A   B

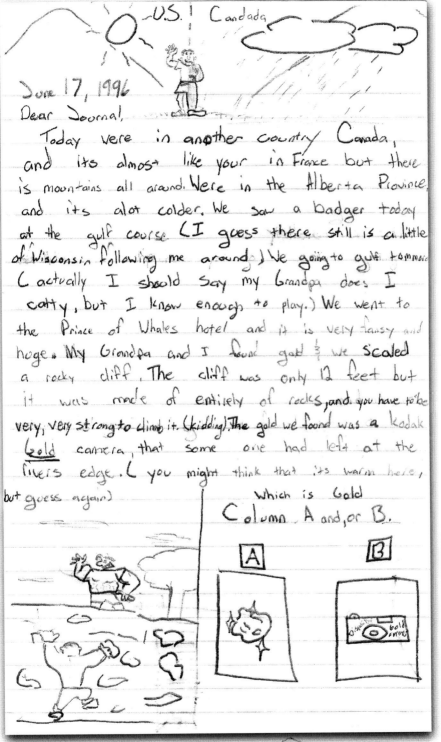

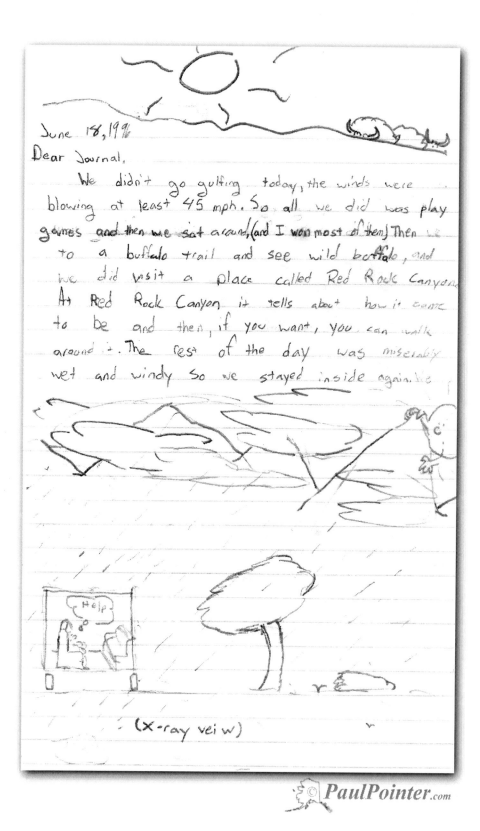

June 18, 1996

Dear Journal,

We didn't go gulfing today, the winds were blowing at least 45 mph. So all we did was play games and then we sat around, (and I won most of them) Then we to a buffalo trail and see wild buffalo, and we did visit a place called Red Rock Canyon. At Red Rock Canyon it tells about how it came to be and then, if you want, you can walk around it. The rest of the day was miserably wet and windy so we stayed inside again.

(x-ray veiw)

June 19, 1996

Dear Journal

Today we drived from Waterton to Two sisters Campground east of Banff. Then we ate lunch, and when I was putting my lettuce on my sandwich There was A big black juicy house fly in my sandwich (but it was squashed and dead) And I almost ate it! After LUNCH I went down to a stream nearby and skipped a few stones (I have a stone that I brought back if you want to see it) Then the rest of the day I explored the area (and I found that these was rats in the outhouses).

looks yumy.

what's that?

June 20, 1996

Dear Journal,

Today we traveled from Waterton park to Jasper and we saw alot of things on the way! Big horn sheep crossing the road and the eating grass, Mt. Goats scaling the rocks on the Mountains, some elk blocking traffic, a black wolf running a cross a pasture, a mule deer minding his own buisness on the side of the road, and some obinoxious ravens just looking for food. We were also at the Columbian Icefeild (also called Athabascan Glaicer). Everythings so expensive! I was going to trade in some American Money (at the bank) to Canadian money, to bring back home to show, and it cost $5 to exchange the money! So if I had $20 I would get $15 back in Canadian, So I said forget it.

June 21, 1996

Dear Journal,

today we traveled from Wisters camp ground in Jasper to Wapiti camp ground in the Jasper area. We did the first wash of the trip! (in a washing machine, I mean) We store up our dirty clothes in a bag and when it is full we "do the wash" (we try not to do it alot because its expensive, it costs about $5.) We had a porcupine cross our path, and I am sure glad grandpa saw it or we would of had a flat tire. We also hiked down Magligne Canyon its like a river that kept digging and digging and it has alot of water falls. The canyon ends & then it leads into Magligne lake, we also then visited Nedicine Lake. The animals we saw today were some bighorn sheep's a male elk that had gigantic horns.

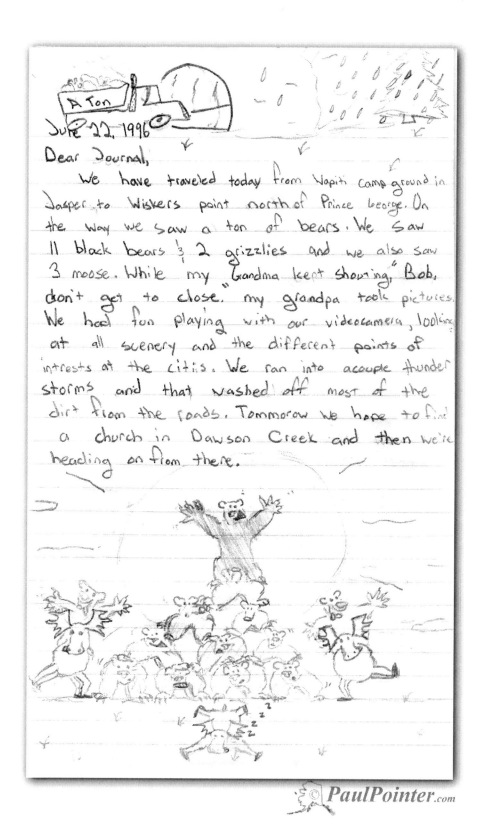

A Ton

June 22, 1996

Dear Journal,

We have traveled today from Wapiti camp ground in Jasper to Wiskers point north of Prince George. On the way we saw a ton of bears. We saw 11 black bears & 2 grizzlies and we also saw 3 moose. While my Grandma kept shouting," Bob, don't get to close," my grandpa took pictures. We had fun playing with our videocamera, looking at all scenery and the different points of intrests at the citis. We ran into acouple thunder storms and that washed off most of the dirt from the roads. Tommorow we hope to find a church in Dawson Creek and then we're heading on from there.

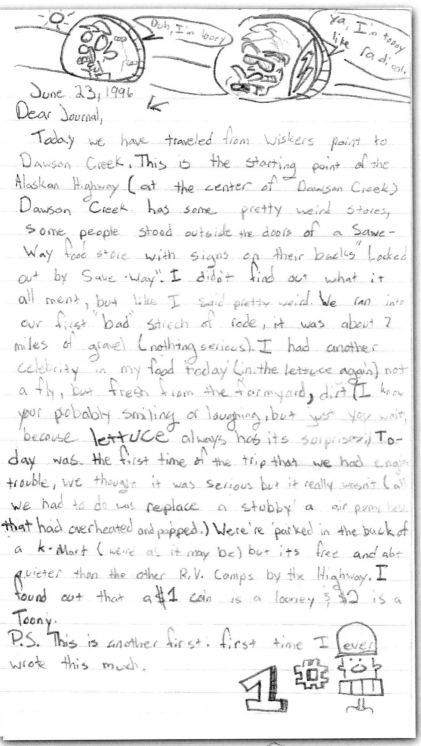

June 23, 1996

Dear Journal,

Today we have traveled from Wiskers point to Dawson Creek. This is the starting point of the Alaskan Highway (at the center of Dawson Creek) Dawson Creek has some pretty weird stores, some people stood outside the doors of a Save-Way food store with signs on their backs "Locked out by Save-Way". I didn't find out what it all ment, but like I said pretty weird. We ran into our first "bad" strech of rode, it was about 2 miles of gravel (nothing serious). I had another celebrity in my food today (in the lettuce again) not a fly, but fresh from the farmyard, dirt (I know your probably smiling or laughing, but just you wait, because **lettuce** always has its surprises.) Today was the first time of the trip that we had engine trouble, we thought it was serious but it really wasn't (all we had to do was replace a "stubby" a air pump hose that had overheated and popped.) We're parked in the back of a k-Mart (weird as it may be) but its free and abt quieter than the other R.V. Camps by the Highway. I found out that a $1 coin is a looney & $2 is a Toony.

P.S. This is another first: first time I ever wrote this much.

June 24, 1996

Dear Journal,

We headed off today from the parking lot of K-Mart to the misquito invaided lot of Buckle up ranch (R.V. pit stop) On the way to the "seatbelt ranch" we had a few, um, let me say problems with the engine. Our air pump hose melted off so we stopped at Mae's kitchen & Ed's garage and got a new one and it worked for the rest of the day (hopefully tommorrow too.) I got an exchange of money today (luckly it wasn't a $5 fee to exchange) At Dawson Creek (where the k-Mart is) there is a MILE POST "0" (like I said yesterday," the starting of the Alaskan Highway.) We are starting it today and it is 1550 mi to Dawson Creek to Fairbanks where our cousins live. We saw a cow moose and a huge beaver "lodge".

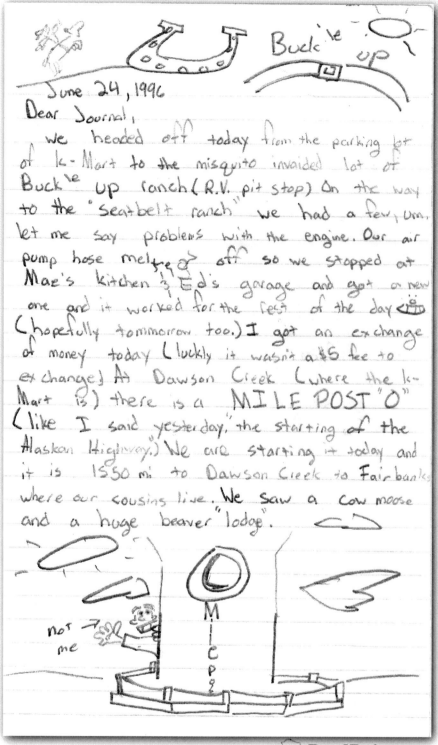

not me

M
i
c
p
q

If you didn't notice

June 25, 1996 " " " sheep
Dear Journal,
   Traviling from Buckle up Ranch to the beautiful turquoius waters of R.V. Wilderness at Muncho Lake, British Columbia. We had engine again! But this time we fixed it for sure, it was E.G.R valve (Exaust, Gas, Recirculation valve) that needed to be replaced. The E.G.R. valve was overheating the tube causing it to melt. On the way to Muncho we saw two caribou (reindeer) a young female, and a large adult male. We also saw a group of stone sheep along the road. Tonights entertainment was Grandpas solo on the recorder (well not quite entertainment but an improvisation of some tunes.)
   P.S. the Muncho gorge is gorgeous! (get it?)

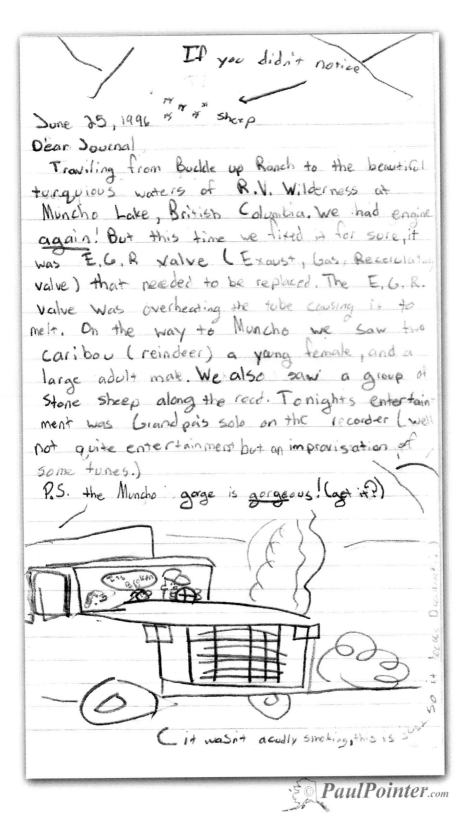

(it wasn't acudly smoking, this is just so it looks Dramatic!)

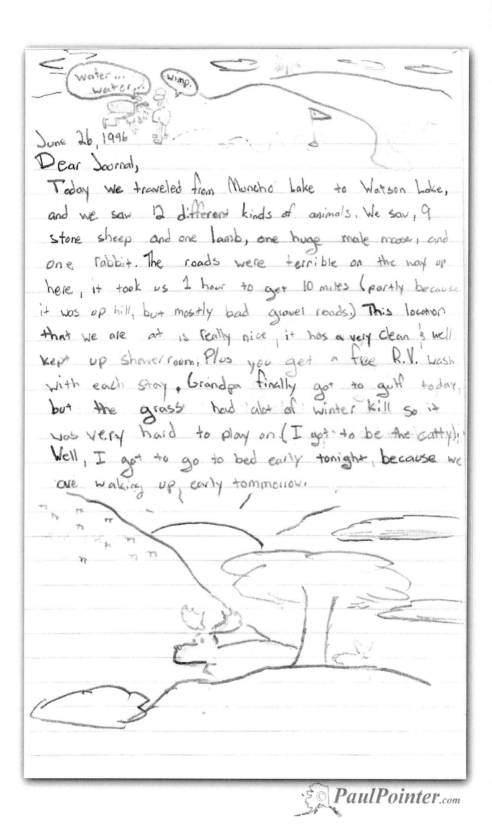

June 26, 1996

Dear Journal,

Today we traveled from Muncho Lake to Watson Lake, and we saw 12 different kinds of animals. We saw, 9 stone sheep and one lamb, one huge male moose, and one rabbit. The roads were terrible on the way up here, it took us 1 hour to get 10 miles (partly because it was up hill, but mostly bad gravel roads.) This location that we are at is really nice, it has a very clean & well kept up shower room; Plus you get a free R.V. wash with each stay. Grandpa finally got to golf today, but the grass had alot of winter kill so it was very hard to play on (I got to be the catty); Well, I got to go to bed early tonight, because we are waking up, early tommorow.

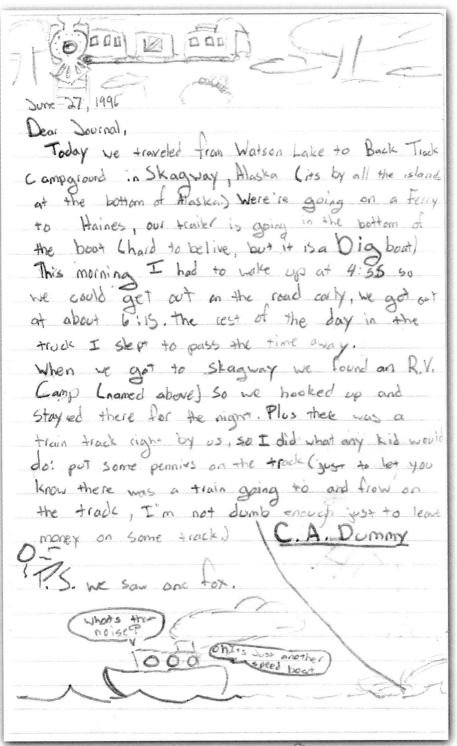

June 27, 1996

Dear Journal,

Today we traveled from Watson Lake to Back Track Campground in Skagway, Alaska (its by all the islands at the bottom of Alaska) We're going on a Ferry to Haines, our trailer is going in the bottom of the boat (hard to belive, but it is a big boat) This morning I had to wake up at 4:55 so we could get out on the road early, we got out at about 6:15. The rest of the day in the truck I slept to pass the time away.

When we got to Skagway we found an R.V. Camp (named above) So we hooked up and stayed there for the night. Plus there was a train track right by us, so I did what any kid would do: put some pennies on the track (just to let you know there was a train going to and frow on the track, I'm not dumb enough just to leave money on some track.)   C.A. Dummy

P.S. We saw one fox.

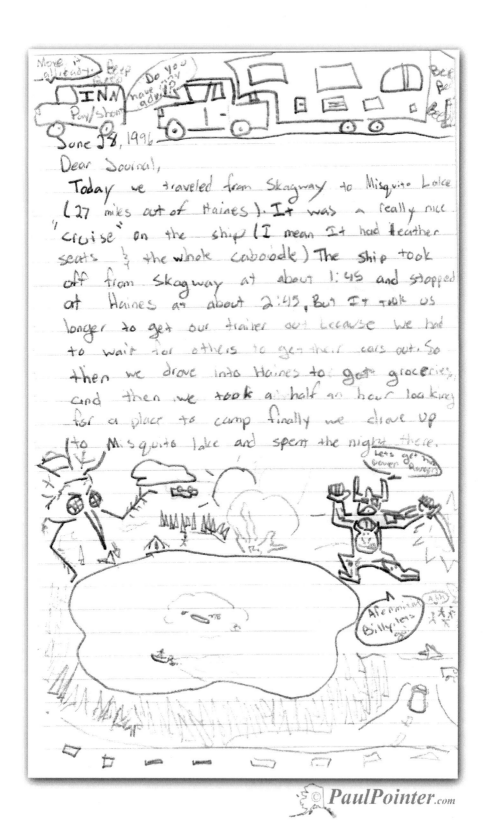

June 28, 1996

Dear Journal,

Today we traveled from Skagway to Misquito Lake (27 miles out of Haines). It was a really nice "cruise" on the ship (I mean It had leather seats & the whole caboodle) The ship took off from Skagway at about 1:45 and stopped at Haines at about 2:45. But It took us longer to get our trailer out because we had to wait for others to get their cars out. So then we drove into Haines to get groceries, and then we took a half an hour looking for a place to camp finally we drove up to Misquito lake and spent the night there.

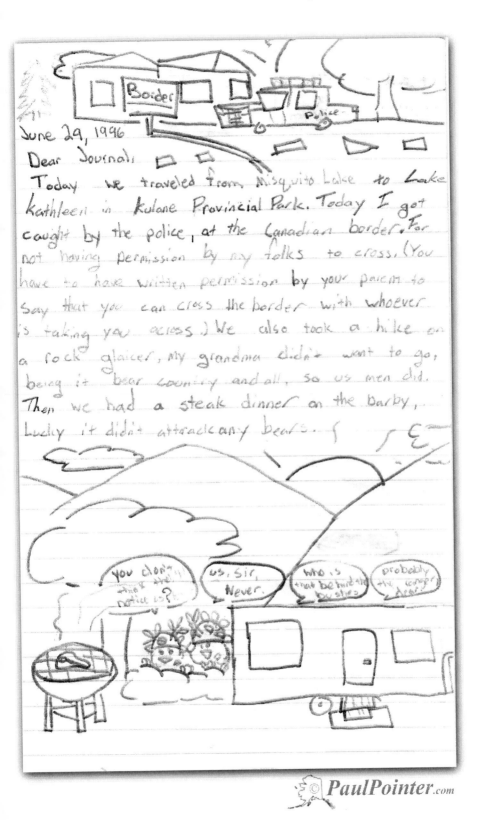

June 29, 1996

Dear Journal,

Today we traveled from Misquito Lake to Lake Kathleen in Kulane Provincial Park. Today I got caught by the police, at the Canadian border. For not having permission by my folks to cross. (You have to have written permission by your parents to say that you can cross the border with whoever is taking you across.) We also took a hike on a rock glacier, my grandma didn't want to go, being it bear country and all, so us men did. Then we had a steak dinner on the barby. Lucky it didn't attrack any bears.

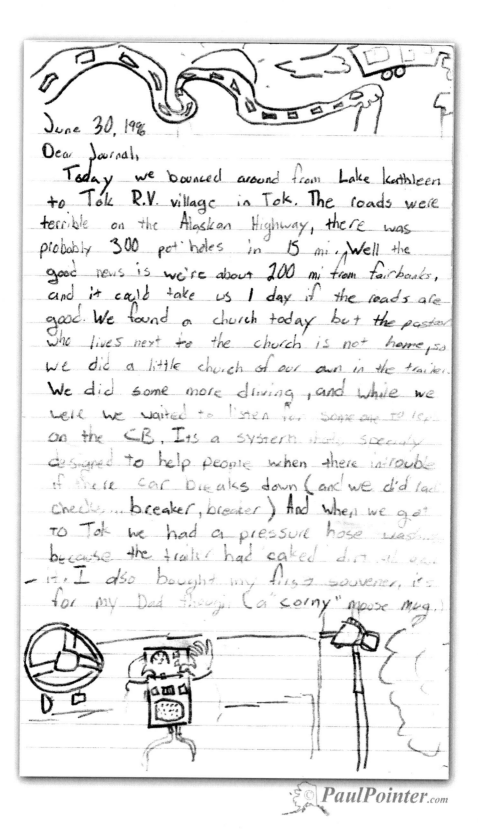

June 30, 1998

Dear Journal,

Today we bounced around from Lake Kathleen to Tok R.V. village in Tok. The roads were terrible on the Alaskan Highway, there was probably 300 pot holes in 15 mi. Well the good news is we're about 200 mi from Fairbanks, and it could take us 1 day if the roads are good. We found a church today but the pastor who lives next to the church is not home, so we did a little church of our own in the trailer. We did some more driving, and while we were we waited to listen for someone to talk on the CB. Its a system that, specially designed to help people when there in trouble if there car breaks down (and we did talk checks... breaker, breaker) And when we got to Tok we had a pressure hose wash because the trailer had caked dirt all over it. I also bought my first souvenir, it's for my Dad though (a "corny" moose mug)

Coley and Larry

July 1, 1996

Dear Journal,

Today the roads were great (but a little dippy) from Tok to Fairbanks. We saw 3 bald eagles, one car on the road that had flipped over, and evedince on the road that one large animal (probably a moose) got hit by a car. Fairbanks is the high-light of my trip, our cousins house is huge. They have 20- or 30 chickens, 10 sled dogs, one house dog, and alot of weird neighbors (tailor, Jimmy & logan) I think I could stay here for the year.

P.S. They also have sega game gear!

Mush Mush

your right he is in mush.

July 2

July 2, 1996
Dear Journal,

I'll just say I played all day b/c thats mostly what I did, I watered the dogs, fed the chickens, rode on the trail, played sega game gear, and watched some movies ...

July 3, 1996
Dear Journal,
   You must feel awfully lonley just sitting
on the same shelf day after day after day,
well you get my point. So I'm just going
to let you sit there, since your getting use
to it (well at least I'll say I played more today)

Not this time

July 4, 1996

Dear Journal,

HAPPY 4th OF JULY!!! Sorry no firecrackers this year (with all the forest fires, they think its a hazard to the trees) But got to watch Jumanji (It was cool)

P.S. four more days until my birthday.

July 5, 1996
Dear Journal,
    I finally memorized all 10 of the dog names (There easier to say than to spell!
Rocky, Nova, Shmernof, Nickita, Covic,
Rusty, Kagles, Graner, troubles, ; Tok. I also
watched D2 the Mighty Ducks.

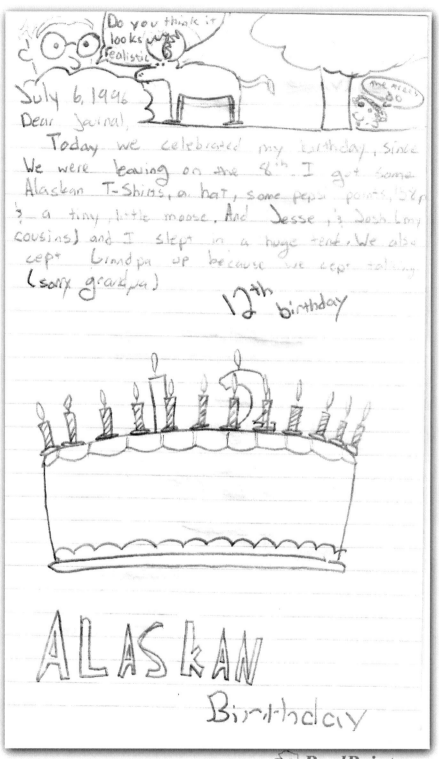

July 6, 1996
Dear Journal,
    Today we celebrated my birthday, since
we were leaving on the 8th. I got some
Alaskan T-Shirts, a hat, some pepsi points, 50¢,
& a tiny, little moose. And Jesse (& Josh (my
cousins) and I slept in a huge tent. We also
cept Grandpa up because we cept talking.
(sorry grandpa)

12th birthday

ALASKAN
Birthday

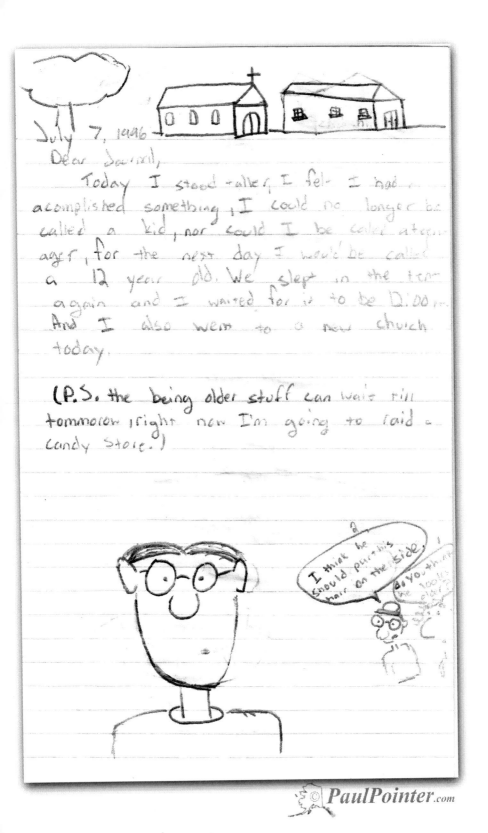

July 7, 1996

Dear Journal,

Today I stood taller, I felt I had acomplished something, I could no longer be called a kid, nor could I be called a teenager, for the next day I would be called a 12 year old. We slept in the tent again and I waited for it to be 12:00 am. And I also went to a new church today.

(P.S. the being older stuff can wait till tommorow, right now I'm going to raid a candy store.)

July 8th

Dear Journal,

Today we traveled from Fairbanks, Alaska to Denali National Park. We're going to stay here on the 10th to the 14th, but first were going to stay at Grizzley Bear about 9 miles away from Denali Park. At Grizzley Bears we took a hike down to the river, checked out the gift shop, and filled up our tank with water. Then we did some more exploring.

P.S its my birthday today!

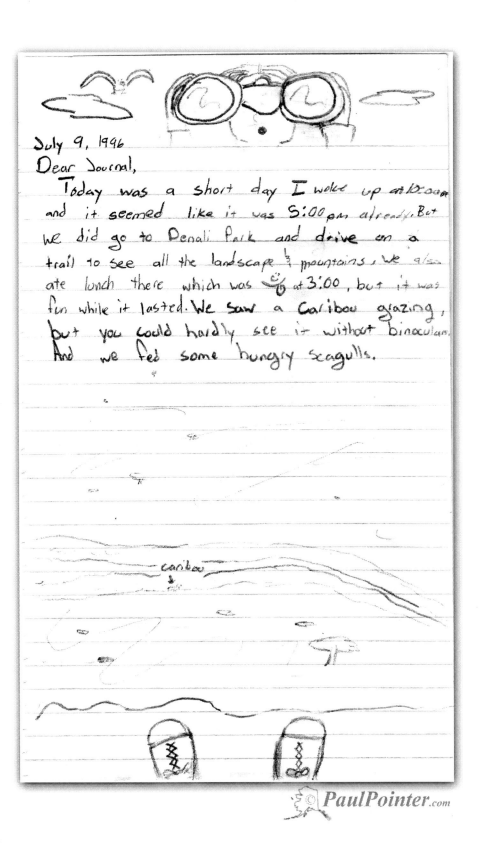

July 9, 1996

Dear Journal,

Today was a short day I woke up at 10:00am and it seemed like it was 5:00pm already. But we did go to Denali Park and drive on a trail to see all the landscape & mountains. We also ate lunch there which was at 3:00, but it was fun while it lasted. We saw a Caribou grazing, but you could hardly see it without binoculars. And we fed some hungry seagulls.

caribou

July 10, 1996

Dear Journal,

Today we went to see a Dog Sled deminstration, it was neat. The girl went on the Dog Sled driving on gravel, kicking it up everywhere as the dogs went at a fast pace of 20-30 mi/h. FUN. Besides that we went to a visitor center and hung around there looking at every thing possible. Then I bought my mom a vase out. I'm not going to tell you the price b/c my moms probably going to read this also.

Just don't drop it, Ma

July 11, 1996
Dear Journal,
 Today we went to alot of Ranger programs today. We went to a speaking about Denali is like a box of chocolates... Bears, & Glaciers. I also went to the Dog Pen again (Finally I got to do something by myself) Then I took some hikes and explored the area.

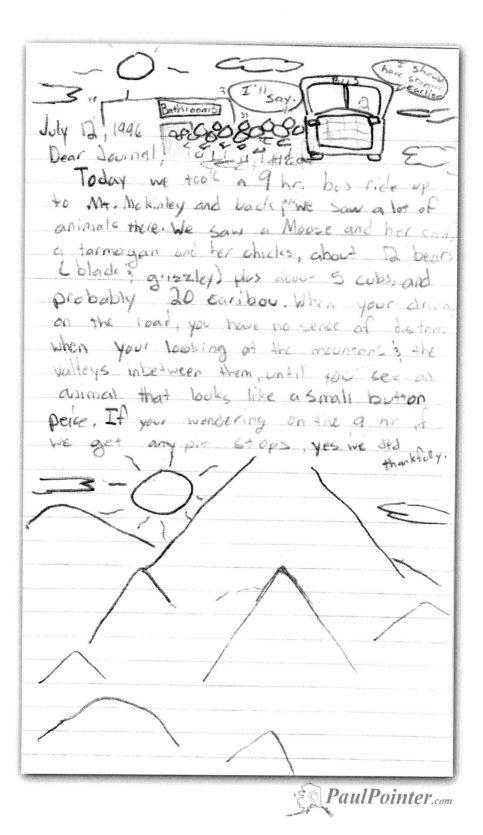

July 12, 1996
Dear Journal,

Today we took a 9 hr. bus ride up to Mt. McKinley and back. We saw a lot of animals there. We saw a Moose and her calf, a tarmagan and her chicks, about 12 bears (black? grizzley) plus about 5 cubs, and probably 20 caribou. When your driving on the road, you have no sence of distence when your looking at the mountens & the valleys inbetween them, until you see an animal that looks like a small button peice. If your wondering on the 9 hr if we get any pit stops, yes we did thankfully.

July 13, 1996

Dear Journal,

Today we left Denali National Park and traveled to Byer's lake in Denali State park. It rained on 1/3 off for ah, an hour or two, so after it was all damp so we couldn't do anything exept stay inside and play games.

Let me out!!!

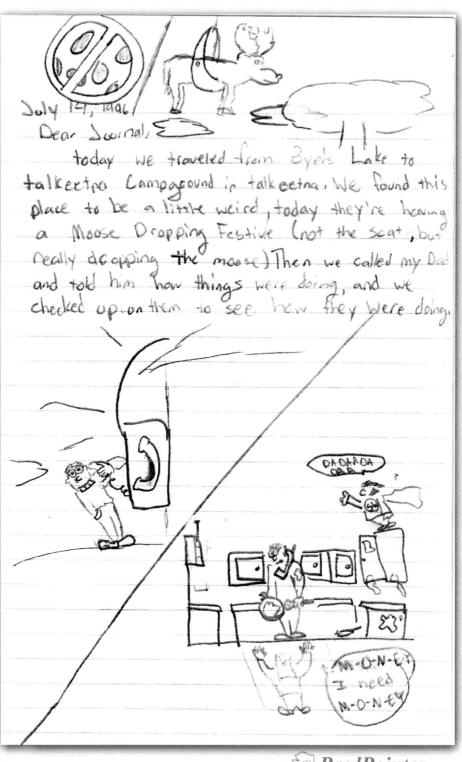

July 14, 1996

Dear Journal,

today we traveled from Byer's Lake to talkeetna Campground in talkeetna. We found this place to be a little weird, today they're having a Moose Dropping Festive (not the scat, but really dropping the moose) Then we called my Dad and told him how things were doing, and we checked up on them to see how they were doing.

Do not let little things descourage you) be strong, and do not fear. Try your best in life for God, He gave you gifts, he wants you to use them for his intentions; do not say "oh, people will laugh at me if I make a mistake God, use that as a building block, learn from your mistakes. If you get a that are in your foot or of a store in your shoe take it out and keep on going. push it aside, if some one laughs at you don't let him get to you b/c th What he wants, he wants you to feel miserable. Same with the Devil) he wants you suffer; he wants the same fate for you, b/c he has to suffer it as well. God is watching over you, he will guide you, if you put your faith in him you will see miracals happen, if theres a barrier in your path jump it, if theres a mountain in your way climb it, God has a plan for you, and even though it didn't work out the way you planned it you'll find it worked out better his way, God knows when your time will come and it we won't be done until he's finished with you. And each time you follow him your building blocks will get higher 3 stronger. So keep on building up your faith and trust for you will need it when he calls

July 14 1996
Byron lake
Denali State Park

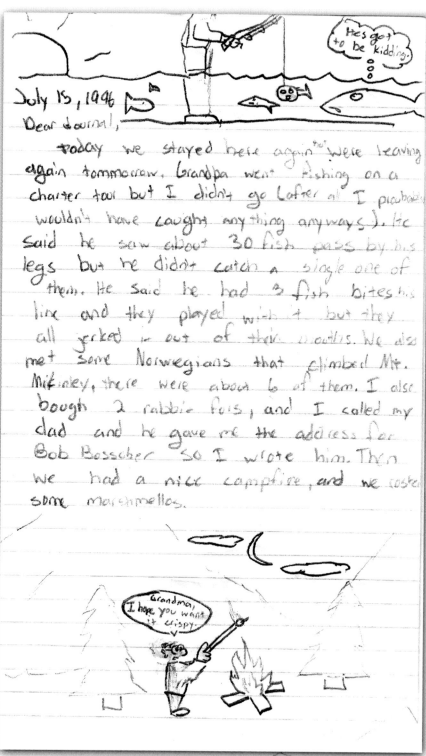

July 15, 1996

Dear Journal,

Today we stayed here again. We're leaving again tommorow. Grandpa went fishing on a charter tour but I didn't go (after all I probably wouldn't have caught anything anyways). He said he saw about 30 fish pass by his legs but he didn't catch a single one of them. He said he had 3 fish bites his line and they played with it but they all jerked it out of their mouths. We also met some Norwegians that climbed Mt. McKinley, there were about 6 of them. I also bough 2 rabbit furs, and I called my dad and he gave me the address for Bob Bosscher so I wrote him. Then we had a nice campfire, and we roasted some marshmellos.

July 16, 1996

Dear Journal,

Today we traveled from Talkeetna to Montana River Campground, by the Montana River. Grandpa caught 2 chum salmon and we ate them for dinner. He snagged one on the tail, and the other on the eyelid. Then we had to clean them (which was fun) and when you push on the heart it beats. Also we saw a panorama of Mt. McKinley and the other mountain ranges beside it.

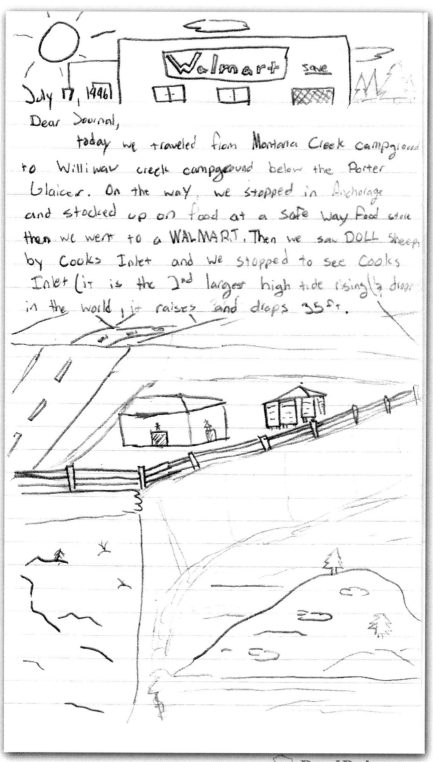

July 17, 1996

Dear Journal,

today we traveled from Montana Creek campground to Williwaw creek campground below the Porter Glacier. On the way, we stopped in Anchorage and stocked up on food at a Safe Way food store then we went to a WALMART. Then we saw DOLL sheep, by Cooks Inlet and we stopped to see Cooks Inlet (it is the 2nd largest high tide rising/ & dropping in the world, it raises and drops 35ft.

July 18, 1996
Dear Journal,

Today we went from Williwaw Campground to the Kenai Princess Campground. We saw a moose this morning with huge racks, he was just minding his own business walking around eating shrubs. Then we went to the Portage Glacier Visitor center and learned about all the different glaciers in the area (there are 10,000 glaciers in the park!) We also learned about the tiny worm creatures in the ice called Ice worms. (the eat the pollen and algey that blows onto the glaciers. We saw a film on glaciers called, The Sound of Glaciers, that was also very magnificent. Then when we got to the campground, Grandpa did the wash while grandpa and I went fishing but there was no fish 🐟 because all the fish went up stream. We finally don't have to dry camp! All the other camps for at least the last week didn't have elec. or they didn't have water only a pump.

July 19, 1996

Dear Journal,

Today we stayed at the same campground
while we waited for our cousins arrival. We are
going to meet them here tonight, and move on
tommorrow morning. But this morning we did
some more wash (we washed the sheets on
our beds) and we ate a delicious breakfast with
doughnuts and we had bannanas and blueberries on
our cereal. After that I explored the gift
shop they had and the motel. The rest of
the day we went fishing (like until five)
And I fell in, I slipped on the path
because it was slanted ⟍⟋ water. Then we went
home (to the trailer) I got cleaned up and we
whatched some of the olympic games. But
after that we relaxed in the motels hot
tub and after that I took a shower.

La La La
La
La

MEN

What is that aweful noise?

I don't know dear.

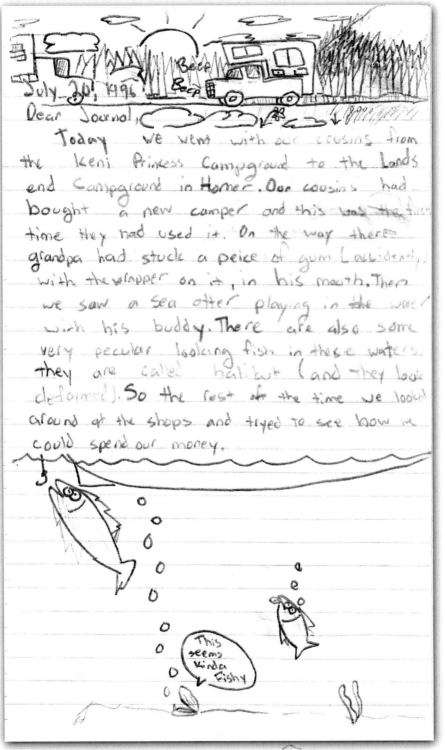

July 20, 1996

Dear Journal,

Today we went with our cousins from the Kení Princess Campground to the Lands end Campground in Homer. Our cousins had bought a new camper and this was the first time they had used it. On the way there grandpa had stuck a peice of gum (accidently) with the wrapper on it, in his mouth. Then we saw a sea otter playing in the water with his buddy. There are also some very peculiar looking fish in these waters. they are called halibut (and they look deformed). So the rest of the time we looked around at the shops and tryed to see how we could spend our money.

This seems kinda Fishy

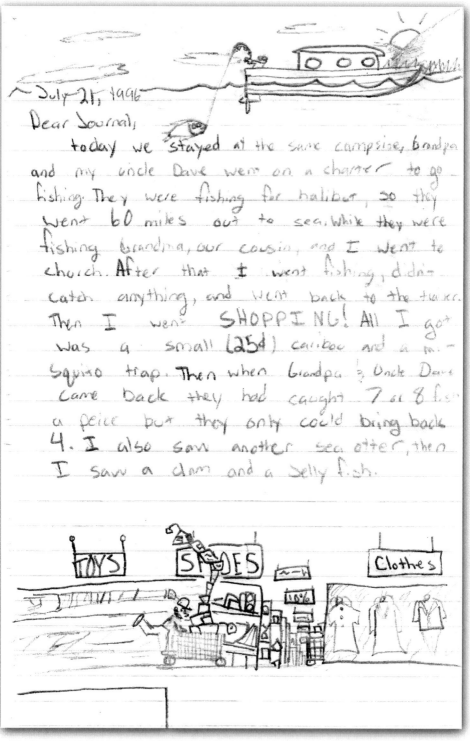

July 21, 1996

Dear Journal,

today we stayed at the same campsite, Grandpa and my uncle Dave went on a charter to go fishing. They were fishing for halibut, so they went 60 miles out to sea. While they were fishing Grandma, our cousin, and I went to church. After that I went fishing, didn't catch anything, and went back to the trailer. Then I went SHOPPING! All I got was a small (25¢) caribou and a mosquito trap. Then when Grandpa & Uncle Dave came back they had caught 7 or 8 fish a peice but they only could bring back 4. I also saw another sea otter, then I saw a clam and a Jelly fish.

TOYS   SHOES   Clothes

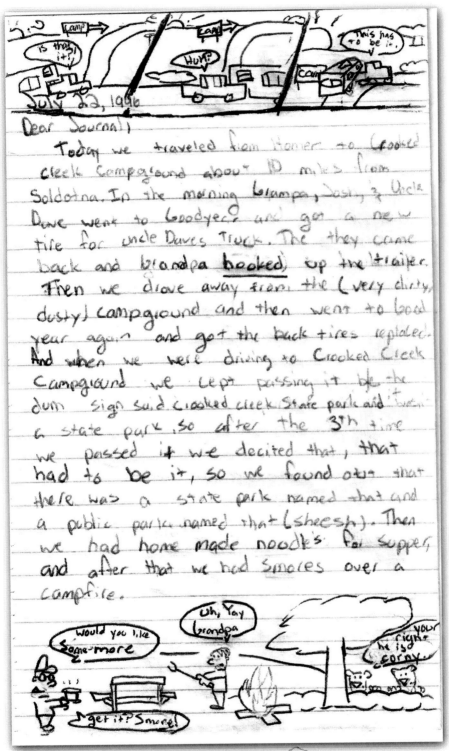

July 22, 1996

Dear Journal,

Today we traveled from Homer to Crooked creek Campground about 10 miles from Soldotna. In the morning Grampa, Josh, & Uncle Dave went to Goodyear and got a new tire for uncle Daves Truck. The they came back and grandpa hooked up the trailer. Then we drove away from the (very dirty, dusty) campground and then went to good year again and got the back tires replaced. And when we were driving to Crooked Creek Campground we kept passing it b/c the dum sign said Crooked creek State park and it wasn't a state park, so after the 3th time we passed it we decided that, that had to be it, so we found out that there was a state park named that and a public park named that (sheesh). Then we had home made noodles for supper, and after that we had smores over a campfire.

Now where is that lake

July 23, 1996

Dear Journal,

Today we left Crooked Creek and went to Hidden Lake Campground (near Cooper Landing 😊). Today was a hectic and very stressful day (for Grandpa anyways). We drove through Soldotna and lost uncle Dave, so we stopped and filled up at a gas station. Then he must have drove past us, but we didn't know it. So we drove up a little ways and stopped at Mom's dad's food store (in the parking lot) and we had to take turns waiting outside so if uncle Dave's truck drove by we had to flag him down (while grandpa looked for them with the truck) Then when grandpa came back we went to the Visitor Center near Cooper Landing (and it was 3 miles away from Hidden Lake Campground) And thats where we popped our tire on the trailer (but thankfully we had a spare) Then mad, upset, & devestated, we went to the Hidden Lake Campground. But there I picked some rasberrys (a whole bag full) and climbed a few cliffs. And Josh & I had a camp fire, then we all went to bed (and Grandpa went to bed with a migraine).

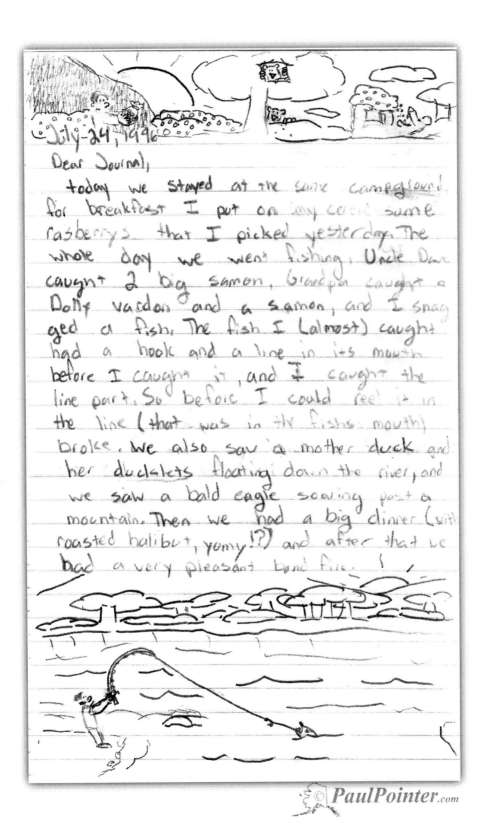

July 24, 1996

Dear Journal,

today we stayed at the same campground. for breakfast I put on my cereal some rasberrys that I picked yesterday. The whole day we went fishing. Uncle Dave caught 2 big samon, Grandpa caught a Dolly vardon and a samon, and I snagged a fish. The fish I (almost) caught had a hook and a line in it's mouth before I caught it, and I caught the line part. So before I could reel it in the line (that was in the fishes mouth) broke. We also saw a mother duck and her ducklets floating down the river, and we saw a bald eagle soaring past a mountain. Then we had a big dinner (with roasted halibut, yomy!?) and after that we had a very pleasant bond fire. !,

July 25, 1996

Dear Journal,

Today Grandpa & Uncle Dave went down to Homer to get the rest of the halibut and to get a new tire. And Aunt Cathy was fishing, so that ment we had to stay the whole day with Grandma. We entertained our selves with a foam miniture airplane for a while, and when we got tired of that we watched some kids hit rocks with a stick. Then we caught and played with some bunnies that were running around. And After that we went to a store, the post office and a grocery store. And after a while we watched the olympics, and then we called Aunt Caroline where Sarah & Laura were and we talked to them (this' was the first time I got to talk to sarah on the whole trip). Then Grandpa & Uncle Dave came back (with aunt Cathy) and then Uncle Dave, Josh, Aunt Cathy (& matty) left, But we stayed. After that we watched some more of the Olympics, then I finally had a shower.

P.S. we traveled to another Campground called Hamiltons Place.

July 26, 1996

Dear Journal,

today we traveled from Hamiltons Place to a city R.V. Park on Resurrection bay at Seward. In the morning we hooked the trailer up & Grandpa put on a new tire (the one he bought on the way back from Homer). At Seward we went to the visitor center and watched 3, 20 min movies. After that we went looking for a charter that would take us to see the Glaciers, and when you get a tour you get an all you can eat buffet. Then we went shopping for some groceries (yummy) and we had to take some cookies back because they were stale. After we got back I did some organizing in my drawers, and then Grandpa & I helped a guy put some rubber on the interior of his hub cap. Then I met a guy (named Scott) that I had seen on the Keni river when Grandpa had caught his fish. Then we looked for his brother, which we found in Scotts Camper. The rest of the day we hung around a Jungle gym. And I wrote my Journal.

Charter

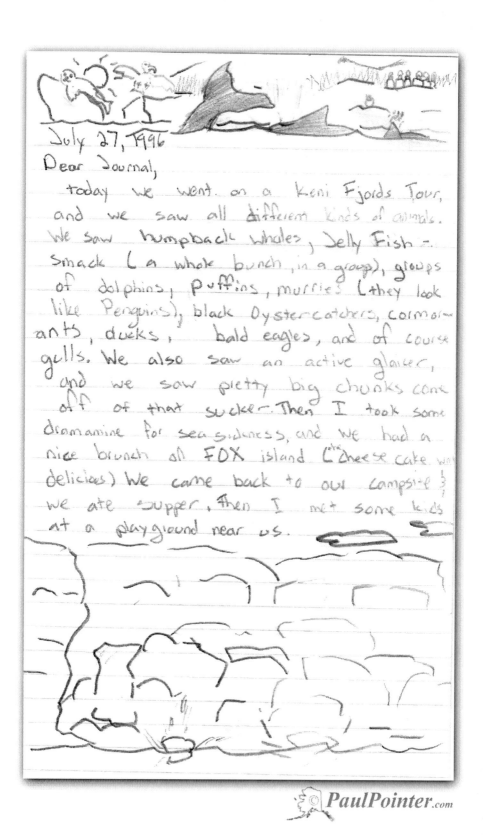

July 27, 1996

Dear Journal,

today we went on a Keni Fjords Tour, and we saw all different kinds of animals. We saw humpback whales, Jelly Fish - Smack (a whole bunch, in a group), groups of dolphins, puffins, murries (they look like Penguins), black Oystercatchers, cormorants, ducks, bald eagles, and of course gulls. We also saw an active glacier, and we saw pretty big chunks come off of that sucker. Then I took some dramamine for seasickness, and we had a nice brunch on FOX island (the cheese cake was delicious) We came back to our campsite & we ate supper, then I met some kids at a playground near us.

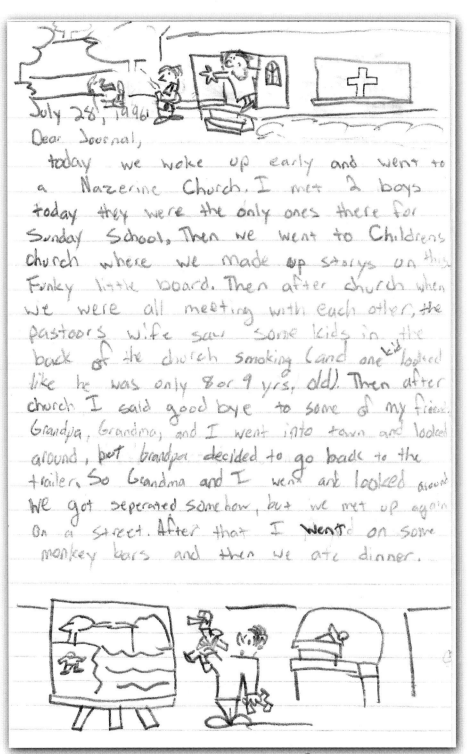

July 28, 1996
Dear Journal,

today we woke up early and went to a Nazerine Church. I met 2 boys today they were the only ones there for Sunday School, Then we went to Childrens church where we made up storys on this Funky little board. Then after church when we were all meeting with each other, the pastoors wife saw some kids in the back of the church smoking (and one kid looked like he was only 8 or 9 yrs. old). Then after church I said good bye to some of my friends. Grandpa, Grandma, and I went into town and looked around, but grandpa decided to go back to the trailer. So Grandma and I went and looked around We got seperated somehow, but we met up again on a street. After that I went'd on some monkey bars and then we ate dinner.

Arch Delux... Mc Donalds

Maybe Late!

July 29, 1996

Dear Journal,

Today we traveled from Seward to Rivers Edge campground in Sutton. At Seward the tide was very low today thats b/c we had a full Moon last night. After a couple hours of driving we stopped at a mall and went over to a McDonalds and got some nice juicy fries with some hamburgers. Then we went browsing inside the mall, and Grandma went shopping. When we arrived at the campground we got electric hook-ups. So we could watch the olympic games, that night we watched the history of World War I. But we had a leak in our sideing and my bed was all wet b/c of it so I had to sleep on the couch.

P.S. It was raining thats how we found out were the leak was.

toys Mall clothes

McDonald M-m-m-m

July 30, 1996

Dear Journal,

Today we left from the damp camp ground, and went to: Sea Otter R.V. Park "Park your R.V. by the Sea..." which was in Valdez. On the way there we saw many glaciers and dazzleing water falls. We got a full hook-up at the R.V. Park and we watched the U.S.A. gymnastic girls and pieformance. We also had another band fire but we had nothing to cook on it. We can see the Oil tankers loading up at a Marine Termanal from the Alaskan pipe line its lights twinkle and flash in the night. I also took a nice hot shower at the building where we registered. Finally.

P.S. In case you didn't know, R.V. means Recreational Veicle.

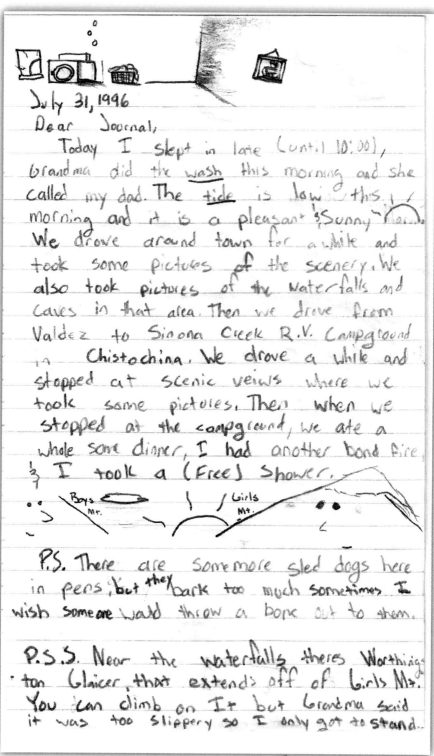

July 31, 1996

Dear Journal,

Today I slept in late (until 10:00), Grandma did the <u>wash</u> this morning and she called my dad. The <u>tide</u> is low this morning and it is a pleasant "Sunny" morning. We drove around town for a while and took some pictures of the scenery. We also took pictures of the waterfalls and caves in that area. Then we drove from Valdez to Sinona Creek R.V. Campground in Chistochina. We drove a while and stopped at scenic veiws where we took some pictures. Then when we stopped at the campground, we ate a whole some dinner, I had another bond fire ⅓ I took a (Free) Shower.

P.S. There are somemore sled dogs here in pens, but they bark too much sometimes I wish someone would throw a bone out to them.

P.S.S. Near the waterfalls theres Worthington Glacier that extends off of Girls Mt. You can climb on It but Grandma said it was too slippery so I only got to stand.

August 1, 1996

Dear Journal,

Today we drove from Chistochina to Gold Rush Campground in Dawson City. We woke up pretty early today and got on the road. Today seemed like an endless drive from the Campground to Nowhere. The roads were terrible, we nearly shook the trailer apart. At first we didn't know there was going to be a strech of road this long, we thought it was only going to be 50 mi long. But when we got to Chicken (it was named that b/c the people who were going to name it Tparmigan didn't know how to spell that name so they named it Chicken), the guy at the gas pump said it was going to be another 120 mi of this road to Dawson City (that freaked Grandpa out) So at Chicken we had a Chicken Sandwhich and we went panning for gold (I got some but Just little flakes). Then we went all the way there (which was forever) and when we got to the begginiing of the city you have to take a ferry across to get there. Then we found out that a dish in The micro wave fell out but didn't break, and the rest of the trailer looked like →

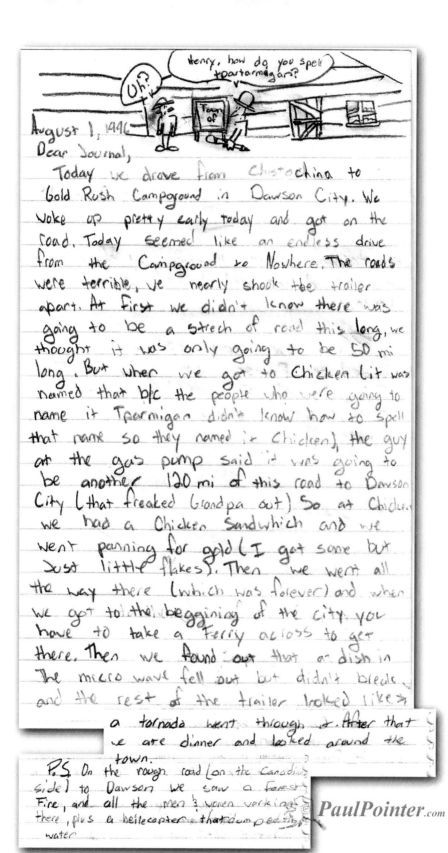

August 1, 1996

Dear Journal,

Today we drove from Chistochina to Gold Rush Campground in Dawson City. We woke up pretty early today and got on the road. Today seemed like an endless drive from the Campground to Nowhere. The roads were terrible, we nearly shook the trailer apart. At first we didn't know there was going to be a strech of road this long, we thought it was only going to be 50 mi long. But when we got to Chicken (it was named that b/c the people who were going to name it Tparmigan didn't know how to spell that name so they named it Chicken) the guy at the gas pump said it was going to be another 120 mi of this road to Dawson City (that freaked Grandpa out) So at Chicken we had a Chicken Sandwhich and we went panning for gold (I got some but Just little flakes). Then we went all the way there (which was forever) and when we got to the beggining of the city you have to take a Ferry across to get there. Then we found out that a dish in the microwave fell out but didn't break and the rest of the trailer looked like a tornado went through it. After that we ate dinner and looked around the town.

P.S. On the rough road (on the Canadian side) to Dawson we saw a Forest Fire, and all the men & women working there, plus a heilecopter that dumped the water.

Aug 2, 96
Dear Journal,
    today we stayed at the campground a little
longer, and took time to see Tom Byrne
recite Robert Services Poems. (He preformed
in front of Roberts small cabin & thats where
he did most of his writings.) I have a picture
to go with it, and a ticket. After that we
walked around and ate lunch. Then we traveled
to Minto Resorts Ltd., R.V. Park   between
Dawson City & White horse   on the Yukon River.
On the way there we saw Bull, a black
Angus, and a black bear with a brown
nose, it was about a 3 yr. old. Then we
drove over the Pelly River, and stopped to
take a look. It was raining really, really hard
when we were driving, and it was almost
in hail form (but lucky it wasn't) So after
we drove around this nifty campground we
found a perfectly level camp site. (a first!)
Then we watched a Thunder storm come in
from 3 mi away which Grandma loves to
see.

Aug 3, 199

Dear Journal,
        Today we filled up with fresh water and dumped the Grey water & the black water. Then we had a pleasent 3 hr, 15 min, & 34 sec drive (b/c I accedently left my stop watch on, when we were timing to put about 15 gal of water in the tank) then we drove about another half an hour. When we got to Whitehoarse we unhitched the truck in a R.V. lot and drove around town. We had a detox meal at Pizza Hut, Oh, it has been such a long time since I've had a Pizza Hut Pizza. Then we went to a grociery store and got some food (I don't know how grandpa could have thought of food after we ate so much.) And they have nifty little carts where you put a quarter in and when your done useing it, you get the coin back (for safety measures I guess) Then we filled up with gas at a Husky Station. Then when we were at Northern Company Trading Station (a gift shop) a ground squirrel was running amuck in the store, so after about 5 min of the store clerk chasing it I through my jacket over him and brought him out side. Then we drove some more and camped at Johnsons X-ing outside of Teslin & along side Teslin River.

P.S. I almost had a fire going in a fire pit but the strong wind blew it out. But Grandpa said it was too windy & so don't try it again, so I didn't.

Aug 4, 1996

Dear Journal,

Today was really cold it was down to 45°F this morning. Plus for some reason our furnace wasn't working (the heater in the trailer) So we were really cold in the morning. Then we drove to Trapper Rays R.V. Park Next to the Liard Hot Springs we wanted to take a dip in the cozy 110°F spring but it was damp and mucky out so we didn't go. On the way here the roads were terrible, pothole city, Like my grandpa said, "These potholes are deeper than an Alaskan out house.". Well it went on for 20 mi and it took us well over 3 hr to drive it. Then we stopped to eat at a large drive of a Gas station. (It was also really cold when we ate so Grandma cooked up some chilly) Then we saw a black bear eating some grub. Then when we got to the campground we looked around (or I should say I did, G & G were in the trailer) Then we played Uno & went to bed.

Hats - Hats - Hats!!

Aug 5, 1996

Dear Journal,
   This morning Grandma & I walked down
to the Liard Hot Springs we would have
went in but Grandpa said we didn't
have enough time (and besides you would
come out smelling like rotten eggs.) Then
we retraced our paths by going through
Muncho Lake, Liard, Toad River, & at Toad
River Lodge they have millions of hats! They
're all on the ceiling (well mabye not Millions
but hundreds & this is where I got a Japan
eze fan from a sale for a present) Then we
drove for a long time (& remembering lots
of the places we were at) then a
caribou heard crossed our path (about 8 or 9
of them) Then we drove alot more and stopped
at a place called Sikanni River Campground
(and we got there at 6 p.m. and we started
off at 9.00 am. This morning) Then I
had a campground and roasted this new
kind of marshmellow (cherry, lemon, & lime flavor)
then we had nice, hot (FREE!!!)
Showers.   H O t !?

   P.S. This is Mud hole city. I mean
mucky.

Aug 6, 1996

Dear Journal,

Today we drove without any destination, we drove & drove & drove until we got Dawson Creek where we checked out tubbys R.V. Park. Grandpa thought about staying here but he would have to wait till tommorow to gulf b/c there was a dark rain cloud coming our way (& there was a swimming pool next door which nobody was at, and the sign said "Swim at your own risk," I can see why.) Then we drove through town (which brought back memories) and took highway 2 that heads toward Edmonton (we also got propane at a IGGIS & we also ate lunch there) We stopped at Mae's kitchen and Eds Garage again (Like on June 24th) where we filled up with Gas (it was a Husky Station, 1 more stamp to Go!) Then we drove more and We saw 2 fawns and one Adult deer, which was intresting. Then we drove more until we got to Wee Links Pitch and putt in Grand Prairie, Alberta. Where Grandpa went Golfing, & we finally got T.V.! Then Grandpa washed the Truck & R.V. and I took Abby for a walk.

Aug 7, 1996

Dear Journal,

Today we headed out of the big city, to our destination Edmonton. We stopped at another Husky station along the way (I finally got all of them stamped for the husky dog.) Today we drove a long ways it didn't seem much, but once you thing about it, it is. We saw another fawn, it was a real smooth, tanned deer. Then when we were coming on the highway into Edmonton a guy gives us the notion to roll down our window. Then after Grandpa rolled down our window, he said, "You have a broken window.", Grandpa thought he just ment a crack, but when we stopped at the campground Glowing Embers R.V. park, sure enough it was the whole window. So Grandpa called a guy and he said "we could have it in tommorow." So we covered it with a plastic table cover, (whatever broke it sure picked a good window, right where my bed is, THANKS.) At the campground Grandma did the wash while Grandpa fiddled with is dish trying to get a good signal (to watch T.V. off the satalite).

Then we called my dad on the phone and said Hello, & I took abby for a walk.

P.S. Were going to the West Edmonton Mall tommorow, The Largest Mall in The World!

P.S.oS'; Grandpa never nuagated a signal from the satalite, shucks.

Edmonton MALL

TOYS Candy Water World Amusement Park

Aug 8, 1996

Dear Journal,

Today I woke up with Grandmas wake up call, "You'd better get up if you want to go to the West Edmonton Mall!" So we got up and ate breakfast and headed off to the Mall. Coming back from the mall was easy but going to it was a different matter. Grandma was reading the map and saying one thing while and meaning another so that confused Grandpa, and we got all screwed up. So Grandma handed it over to me and Grandpa & I both figured out where it was. In the mall everything was so expensive, it cost $30 to go in the water park for half of a day ($20 American). But we got to see some dolphins in a tank (3) they seemed awful lonely though (or board) then we saw the Amusment park, and the roller coasters. It looked so cool, but it cost $7 to ride it. So around lunch time we left, and ate in the trailer. Then Grandpa played golf and Grandma & I stayed. I played on a playground for awhile and walked around looking for pepsi points (I have 225 already) Then we had our window repaired, and we ate supper. I took Abby for a walk again & I met the same people from New Hampsire that I met on July 26th.

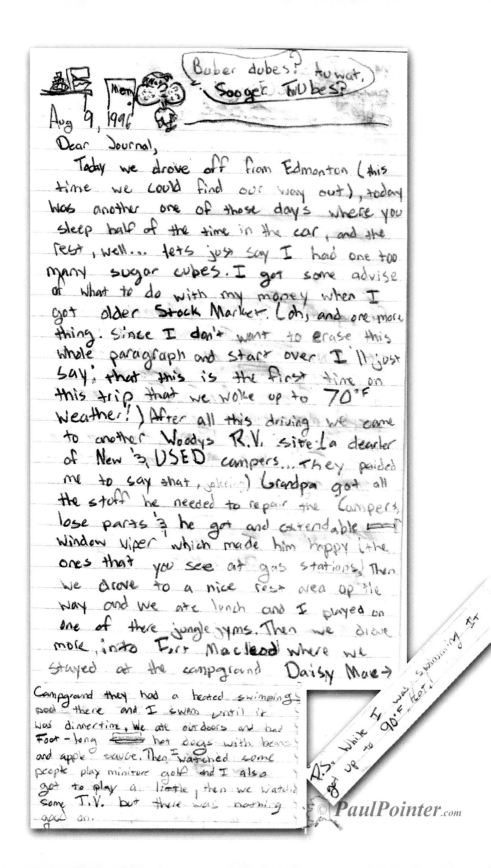

Buber dubes? tu wat, Soogec TUbes?

Mem 1996

Aug 9, 1996

Dear Journal,

Today we drove off from Edmonton (this time we could find our way out), today was another one of those days where you sleep half of the time in the car, and the rest, well... lets just say I had one too many sugar cubes. I got some advise of what to do with my money when I got older Stock Market. (oh, and one more thing. since I don't want to erase this whole paragraph and start over, I'll just say: that this is the first time on this trip that we woke up to 70°F weather!) After all this driving we came to another Woodys R.V. site (a dealer of New & USED campers... They paided me to say that, jokeing) Grandpa got all the stuff he needed to repair the campers lose parts & he got and extendable Window viper which made him happy (the ones that you see at gas stations) Then we drove to a nice rest area up the way and we ate lunch and I played on one of there jungle gyms. Then we drove more, into Fort Macleod where we stayed at the campground. Daisy Mae →

Campground they had a heated swimming pool there and I swam until it was dinnertime. We ate outdoors and had foot-long hot dogs with beans and apple sauce. Then I watched some people play miniture golf and I also got to play a little, then we watched some T.V. but there was nothing good on.

P.S. While I was swimming it got up to 90°F HOT!

© PaulPointer.com

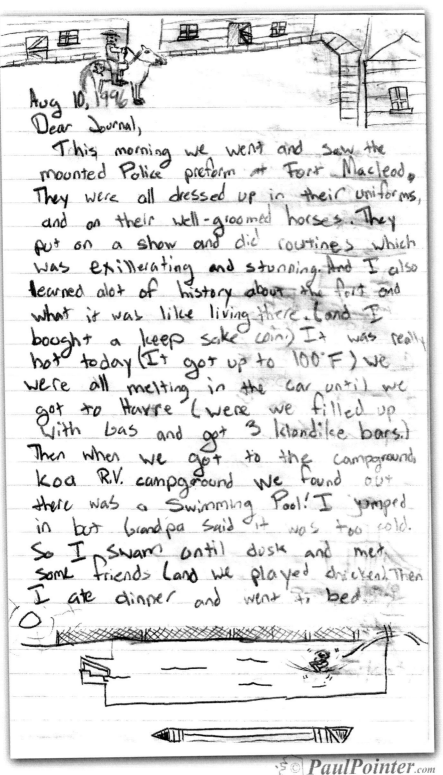

Aug 10, 1996

Dear Journal,

This morning we went and saw the mounted Police preform at Fort Macleod. They were all dressed up in their uniforms, and on their well-groomed horses. They put on a show and did routines which was exillerating and stunning. And I also learned alot of history about the fort and what it was like living there. (and I'm bought a keep sake coin) It was really hot today (It got up to 100°F) we were all melting in the car until we got to Havre (were we filled up with gas and got 3 klondike bars.) Then when we got to the campground, KOA R.V. campground We found out there was a swimming Pool! I jumped in but Grandpa said it was too cold. So I swam until dusk and met some friends (and we played chicken.) Then I ate dinner and went to bed.

Aug 11, 1996
Dear Journal,

today I woke up rather early and got ready, IT turned out to be another HOT, HOT, Day, but we had air conditioning in the truck. We saw 3 or 4 antelope just loping around, "Oh, give me a home..." We stopped at Tioga today to camp (like last time, it was free) I did some more running around on a playground near by, then I went swimming again! (1.25) It was so cool. (1/3 the water) There was a diving board that was 10ft high (which was really fun to dive off of after you landed on your back.) I swam for 2 hr and then I went back to the trailer. Then I ran around some more and after that I hit the sack.

P.S. No baseball game.

Pool

Pool, pool...

Aug 12, 1996
Dear Journal,
        today we left from Tioga, we did the
chores for this morning and then headed
off to Crookson central park in Minnisota. On
the way their we had stopped for lunch
at a gas station, then we took a
very long drive to Minnisota. When we
had stopped at Minnisota I. was really,
really, Hot!!!!! I went around and checked
out the campground, I found out there was
another swimming pool there (olympic size)
(7:00-8:45=$1.) so I waited for that
time to come, hanging around, a beating
the heat. Then we tryed to get our dish
working (no luck, for T.V) but we had local
t.V. (Bob Dole)-speech). Then I went
to the pool, and jumped off an even
higher diving board. Then went back after
swimming for an 1 hr's 45 min. We
called my and told him we would be
at the cottage tomanorrow (Lord →
willing) Thus will end my Journal after
we get home and so will end our
long journey.   OOOOO size

© PaulPointer.com

Aug 13, 1996
Dear Journal,

Today we drove from Crookston to the cottage. It seemed like forever when we were driving so I thought about what it would be like when I got back home. We stopped at the same place as we did when we were coming up. Grandpa picked some choke berries there before we ate, and then after we ate we hit the road. We stopped and filled up with gas at a cenex, and up the road aways we had dumped our sewage (and I found 4 pepsi points.) Then when we were in Wisconsin the driving was forever on going, the minutes seemed like hours and the hours seemed like days. But we finally we got back to the cottage, then we had to back our trailer down the whole driveway, and the fun part was that I was in my shorts and the misquitos were killing me! But we finally got it parked the way we wanted it and then we went inside. We ate a nice supper and a wonderful desert. Then to our surprise Sarah, Laura, & Dad came that night. →

I gave B̶L̶O̶O̶D̶

We told how everything was and how we were doing & we exchanged gifts. (I got a T-shirt, a fruit roll up & a cool pair of sunglasses) Then we watched some T.V. & went to bed. Our trip has finnally ended our Couragoos Voage has stopped I plan to do it again some day ⟹, but Grandpa & Grandma surley not.

－Paul Pointer－ (Grandpa

was accompanied by Amy & Robert Pointer & Grandma)

Theres a land where the mountains are nameless, and the rivers all run God knows where; There are lives that are erring and aimless, and deaths that just hang by a hair. There are hardships that nobody reckons; There are valleys unpeopled and still; There's a land - oh, it beckons and beckons, And I want to go back - and I will.

－Robert Service－

P.S. we also saw 4 vultures.

Traveled 9,884.5 miles round trip.

Portage Valley

CHUGACH
Nationd Forest

Kenai Princess Lodge
overlooking the kenai River

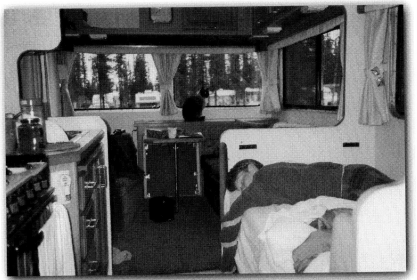

GUEST

Guest Tag from the Church in Fairbanks.

Secret Travel Notes
(with correlating dates)

(June 29th)

(July 3rd)

(July 6th)

(June 26th)

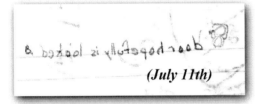

(July 11th)

(July 19th)

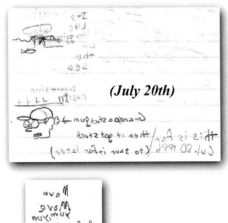

(July 20th)

(July 23rd)

(July 21st)

(July 24th)

Secret Travel Notes 2
(with correlating dates)

(July 26th)

(July 28th)

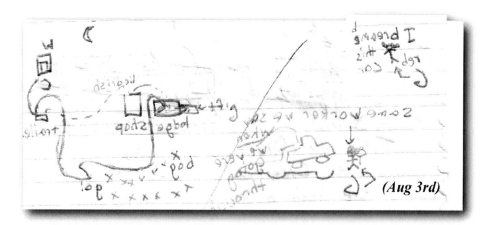

(Aug 3rd)

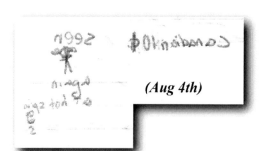

(Aug 4th)

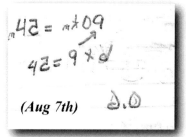

(Aug 7th)

(Aug 8th)

(Aug 9th)

Secret Travel Notes 3
(with correlating dates)

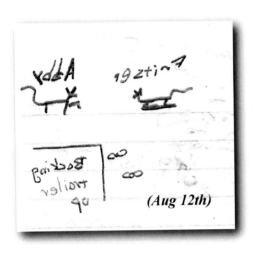

(Aug 12th)

(Aug 10th)

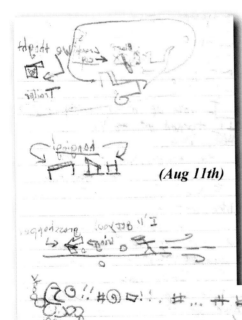

(Aug 11th)

TRAVEL
(links & recommendations)

North Pole, AK- a must see if you are this far NORTH!
(http://www.northpolealaska.com/)

Arctic Circle, AK- from the northern lights to the Trans Alaska Pipeline
(http://www.northernalaska.com/aurora.cfm)

Yukon Museums - Gold Mining and exploration adventures!
(http://www.yukonmuseums.ca/)

British Columbia - Untouched natural beauty
(www.hellobc.com/)

Chevy Trucks - Alaska Tough. Wouldn't travel in anything else.
(www.chevrolet.com/)

P2PRODUCTIONS.COM

©*PaulPointer.com*

Paul Pointer was born in a small
dutch/germanic town in Wisconsin.

Paul loved reading & being read books
by his mother, grandmother and father.
He also enjoyed illustrations , especially
ink mediums.

This is Paul's third book,that he
created in his sixth grade summer (1996).